# BORN
# A
# LOSER

## CORY LOSIER

DOVE

PUBLISHING HOUSE

Requests for permission should be addressed to:

Dove Publishing House
WWW.DOVEPUBLISHINGHOUSE.COM

Hardcover ISBN: 978-1-960807-16-8
Paperback ISBN: 978-1-960807-15-1

# CONTENTS

# DEDICATION

I would like to first dedicate this book to Jesus Christ, my Lord and Savior. Without Jesus, I would not be here at all, let alone walking in freedom where I am now. His grace, mercy, and love have changed my life.

To Christina, my wife, as well as my boys, you have brought me happiness, joy, and a fullness in my heart that no words can describe.

Also, to my dad, mom,and sister and to all of the rest of my family including all of my aunts, uncles, and cousins. I became a prodigal son and left you all for twenty years. I hope reading this book helps you get to know the real me.

My reason behind writing this book was for all addicts, family members of addicts, and those whom are still in prison. I hope by reading this book you will be given hope.

# WARNING: RAW TRUTH

I want to go ahead and say a few things now. Methamphetamine addiction was the worst and hardest thing that has ever happened to me in my whole life. I could not stop. No matter what. No matter whom I hurt. I lost everything and everyone, over and over, until I had nothing left. I tell the hard truth in detail in these pages. When I was in the depths of my addiction, I had no hope, and no one could tell me anything. When someone tried to offer help, I immediately dismissed them with the belief that they didn't know how deep I was. I thought it was too late for me. After all, I had never known anyone to quit and stay clean. I knew older guys who had done it all their life who died doing it. I know there are men and women reading this who are still trapped in addiction and who don't believe they can ever get out. I know there are mothers, fathers, brothers, and sisters who don't believe their loved ones can ever escape. I am writing the raw truth so that no matter how deep someone may be, they can see that there is a way out. If you think your loved one is too deep to ever get out, keep reading. Keep praying. If God can save me, He can save anyone.

My intention in this book is to share in detail many of my experiences as a meth addict over the years in order to create validity with any true addict out there. When I was out there, as deep as I was, I would not listen to anyone, especially if they hadn't been there themselves. I absolutely have been to the bottom of the rabbit hole, and I need the readers of this book who think that they are too deep or too far gone to know, because of my story, that they are not. I also want the moms, dads, brothers, and sisters of their loved one who is an addict to know without any doubt that the one they love, for whom they are praying daily, is absolutely not too far gone. Anyone who has been where I have been will know without any doubt that I have been where they are because of the things I share. I will say it again: Keep praying. If God can save me, He can save anyone.

## CHAPTER 1

# THE BEGINNING

When I was born, my last name was Loser. Yes, literally. L-O-S-E-R. Crazy, right? Of course, it was only spelled like that, not pronounced like that. My grandparents and parents always pronounced it with a long *O*. How in the world this ever happened I don't know. I may not ever know. My grandpa even wore a leather belt with "LOSER" written across the back; it was clearly visible with his shirt tucked in. Now, I know many of you are likely Googling that last name right now. There aren't a lot of us, but you will quickly be able to find it.

The problem is that no matter how my family and I said it was pronounced, it was still spelled *Loser*. Growing up with this last name was very difficult, to say the least.

Everyone made fun of me for it. The other kids did, and even the teachers did. On the first day of every school year in a brand-new class, the first thing the teacher would do is the roll call. They would go down a list, speaking out loud everyone's first and last name in alphabetical order. It was inevitable. The closer they got to *L*, the more I slumped in my chair. I could feel my face getting hotter by the second. Then it would happen. "Cory Loser?" The entire class would break out into laughter.

Most of the time, even the teacher did. Then came the worst part. Not only did I have to raise my hand to let her know I was there, but also, when the teacher asked if this was spelled correctly, I would have to say yes in front of the whole class. Everyone was still looking at me, talking about me, and laughing. Kids would come up to me throughout the day and ask me, "Is your name really Loser?" My normal response was, "Well, it's spelled like *loser*, but it's pronounced *Loser*." That never helped. It was a running joke every day of every year. Some teachers would even pronounce it wrong on purpose after I told them the correct way. In the Loser household, we always knew when a salesman was calling. When we picked up the phone, they would ask, "Is Mr. Loser there?" All of our mail said *Loser*. Every bill, every debit card—everything.

I thought about playing football, and I think I might have been really good, but very early on I realized that if I did, *Loser* would be on the back of my jersey. Can you imagine the ridicule? What if I wasn't good at all? I would go down in history as the biggest Loser that ever played. Of course, looking back on it now, if I had been really good, I may even have become famous. A winner with the last name of Loser! The enemy is really good at using things against us, but God is even better at using things for us. Even things that don't seem like they could ever be good. Unfortunately, at the time, I had no idea I even had an enemy. It would be many years before I learned this.

I hated school. I dreaded every day, because all day every day I got made fun of and laughed at. Not only for my last name, but also for my teeth. My teeth were stained yellow from drinking well water, and they were also crooked. It never stopped. It was a nightmare. Deep down, I always felt like I had so much potential. I had always been physically strong and was overall athletic. I knew if I played sports I would be great, but I never even tried. Not even one time. I wanted to stay as far away from any spotlight as I could. I wasn't about to intentionally usher in another opportunity to get made fun of for my last name, probably even by the coach. No way!

By the time I got to sixth grade, my self-esteem was very low. I was definitely interested in girls by then, but I lacked the confidence to talk to any. I had been emotionally beat up for years, and I was tired of it. All those years of being made fun of had taken a toll. I was fed up. One day, a kid who was bigger than me and part of the popular crowd was making fun of me, and I ended up talking some trash back to him. Before I knew it, I had agreed to fight him after school. It did not take long before the whole school knew about it. I was so mad that it didn't even matter how scared I was. I had never been in a fight before. I wanted to finally teach someone a lesson for making fun of me. Maybe then it would stop.

All day, I was secretly hoping the whole scenario would just go away. Maybe he would forget. No such luck. As soon as the bell rang, everyone immediately started talking about it. A large crowd gathered around me as I walked out of the school. And by large crowd, I mean about half the school. I decided to go for it. I started walking toward the field. I could see my opponent not far away. Once we got to the back part of the field, the crowd automatically made a circle around us, creating a boxing ring. There was cheering and shouting as we started to circle each other. I made the first move. There was punching, kicking, throwing, and rolling. I ended up winning the fight in front of the whole school. All his friends saw, and that night I was feeling pretty good about it. I was sure that from here on out, no one was going to make fun of me again. To my surprise, the only thing that changed was that even more people knew who I was! Ugh!

The torment continued. At least this was my last year of elementary school, and I would be starting a new school for junior high the next year. Maybe things would be different. However, things were not different. Everything just got worse.

# CHAPTER 2

# MY FAMILY

M y family was just my mom, my dad, me, and my little sister. I have a lot of fun memories from my early childhood, including camping trips, boating, Go-Karts, dirt bikes, and exploring creek beds. My parents have always been together, and they remain married to this day. My little sister Lindsay, unlike me, has always been pretty good about not getting into trouble. There was a short time when she did as a teenager, but that was it that I know of. I wish I had been a much better big brother. I tried early on, but I really failed. I was basically nonexistent most of the time, and eventually she didn't want me around anyway—and rightly so. She is an amazing sister who is so fun to be around and full of life, but my choices stole from her the opportunity to have a big brother. I will take this opportunity to say that I truly regret the lost time with her and consider it one of the most valuable things I've lost in my life. You can never get back the time you lose with someone. Once it passes, it is gone forever. You can make a decision to start now and spend as much time as possible with your sister, your brother, your dad, your mom, your daughter, or your son going forward, but you can't go back. So please, cherish every moment with the ones you love from this moment on.

# CHAPTER 3

# EARLY TROUBLE

W hen I was about twelve years old, I went to a flea market with my parents. I bought a ten-inch knife with a belt and sheath. After we got home, for whatever reason, I thought it was a good idea to go to the nearby creek with the knife around my waist and a Jason mask on (from the movie *Friday the 13th*). After messing around down there for a while, I noticed some large piles of dirt at a construction site nearby. Again, I had a great idea. I climbed to the top of the hill, Jason mask still on and knife in hand. A few minutes later, I saw in the distance multiple police cars with lights and sirens on, all coming my direction.

My first instinct was to run to the creek and follow the creek to the backyard of a vacant house I knew of, then cut through to my street undetected and get inside my house. I quickly ran down to the creek and was headed through the tunnel under the road. I was looking down, trying not to trip over all the rocks. Suddenly, I heard, "FREEZE!" That's exactly what I did. There was a cop with his gun drawn and pointed at me. He told me to take off the mask. I did. Then he told me to take the knife and throw it behind me. I did. He then put me in handcuffs and into the back of the police car. I remember being so scared. They drove me to my house and told my parents, who confiscated the mask and knife. I'm sure I was grounded at least.

This would end up being the first of many times I wound up in the back of a police car.

# CHAPTER 4

# DRUGS IN THE BEGINNING

As I mentioned, I had hoped that I would stop getting made fun of in junior high, but I didn't. By the time I was thirteen or fourteen, I was already smoking cigarettes and marijuana, drinking alcohol, and snorting cocaine. All I cared about was having fun. No one in the drug world cared about my last name or my crooked and stained teeth. Everyone was just having fun. For me, drugs were the best thing going. My cousin and I would have our unsuspecting parents drop us off at one place, and from there we would go wherever we wanted. There were no cell phones back then. We had free reign.

Looking back, I didn't know who I was or who I wanted to be. I just didn't want to be me. In the beginning, for me, drugs made life better. I soon forgot about any childhood dreams I had of becoming an actor or a musician. In fact, I forgot about anything other than drugs, including what was most important: my family.

I didn't know anything about God at that time. My family didn't really go to church, and they definitely didn't talk about God. However, even way back then, God was already trying to get my attention. At that time, I had a friend who I thought was the coolest guy I had ever known. He had long hair, played guitar, and listened to music I had never heard. I remember wanting to be like him. In reality, he was a good kid starting down the wrong road just like me. I'll never forget how he came to my parents' house for dinner once, and I ended up choking on an olive. I was choking and struggling to breathe, and he blurted out, "Breathe through the hole, man!" I'm pretty sure I spit it out, because I laughed.

I was spending the night at his house one night. I had hung out there plenty of times before as well. I liked his whole family. There was something different about them. I didn't know why I was drawn to them at the time. His family ate healthy food and worked out. I remember liking that, and it inspired me. They even ate vegetable sandwiches. They also went to church. Although my friend was doing drugs just like I was, his family was serving the Lord. I didn't even know what that meant.

One night, he and I snuck out of his window, and off we went in the middle of the night. We walked a couple of miles. I have no idea where we were going. We would sneak out all the time, me from my house and he from his. We would meet up and do ridiculous things like light firecrackers in people's mailboxes. As always, we were smoking cigarettes and weed. However, on this particular night, after about twenty minutes, his dad pulled up out of nowhere and told us to get in the car. We did. My friend asked how he found us, and his dad said, "God showed me where you were." I had never heard anyone say anything like that. He then told me that the next time I snuck out of my house I would get caught. I expected him to tell my parents, but he never did.

The next night, I snuck out of my parents' house again. "I'm not going to get caught," I thought. "I'll take every precaution." I would wait patiently until I heard my dad snoring loudly. I would wait until the air conditioning unit would kick on outside my window so the dogs next door wouldn't hear me over the noise and bark. Then I would slip out and go past my parents' window around the other side of the house and jump the fence there. It worked; I was out. I remember I walked around for a couple of hours in the middle of the night. Then I came back home. I went back in the same way. This time, though, as I walked past my parents' window, I noticed a TV set was on. "Oh, no!" I thought. I convinced myself that I just didn't notice it on the way out. I sat there and waited for the air conditioning unit to kick back on, and then I quickly walked up to my window. As I slowly started to slide my window open, there was a sudden loud noise that sounded like clanking metal falling to the floor! Had I left something in the window? No, of course not. It would have fallen on the way out. My heart racing, I jumped behind the air conditioning unit and ducked down. Immediately there was a flashlight beam shining all around. It happened too fast for one of my parents to get from their room to mine. They had to have been waiting in my room already. Seconds later, I heard the automatic garage door opening and a car pulling out.

I had to think of something fast. I took off all my clothes except my underwear, and then I jumped over the fence and ran down the street after my parents' car. I caught up and knocked on the window to stop them. It was my mom. I told her I was just in the backyard the whole time. I thought she would believe me since I had no clothes on. Unfortunately, they had already looked there. I was caught. There was nothing I could do but take the consequences. It was the most trouble I had been in up to that point. They were furious. They took the door to my room off the hinges that night. I'm pretty sure I got spanked for the last time in my life that night as well. I remember lying there, thinking about what my friend's dad had told me about getting caught the next time I snuck out and that God had told him that. They moved away not too long after that, so I lost contact with him. I wanted to share this story because if you are a parent, I want you to know God is speaking to your kids, even when they are young. I remember. Even in the midst of being high, I remember. As soon as I started going astray, God began to show

Himself to me. He cares about your son. He cares about your daughter. He is not willing that any should perish.

At this point, my life was still manageable. No one, including my family, really knew anything about my new lifestyle. I was still in school, and somehow I was passing, although barely.

## CHAPTER 5

# THE BEGINNING
# OF THE END

When I was fifteen years old, I was introduced to methamphetamine. I felt like Superman. I felt smarter and stronger. Up to this point I had generally been what I would consider a bit lazy and unmotivated to do basically anything. After taking meth, I was no longer lazy. I wanted to do everything and learn everything. The problem was, I wanted to learn everything about drugs. Once meth came on the scene, that's all I ever did. Every day, all day. I loved it. I was constantly meeting new people, and I was absolutely intrigued by this drug, the people who did it, and the lifestyle in general. For a while, I was able to hold jobs here and there, just long enough to get some money in my pocket. I would use that to buy enough to sell and make just enough money to support my habit. A guy whom I looked up to at the time said to me, "You don't know what you are getting into, but by the time you find out, it will be too late." I didn't know what he meant at the time, but I do now. At sixteen years old, I dropped out of school. I was already skipping most of my classes anyway. It was my first year of high school. I did at least get my GED a couple weeks afterward.

## CHAPTER 6

# PHARMACY

When I was seventeen years old, I got a job as a pharmacy technician. Boy, was this the wrong job for me! I quickly figured out how things worked there, and before long, I was stealing all kinds of pills. There were huge crates lying on the ground, full of narcotics that were expired and going to be disposed of. So I disposed of them. On all my smoke breaks and my lunch break, I would fill up my pharmacy jacket pockets and haul them out to my car and stash them. Hundreds of Xanax bars, Lortab, Vicodin, and all kinds of other drugs.

I was taking the Xanax bars daily, and I would black out for long periods of time, sometimes even whole days. I would come to and not know what I had done or said for however long I had been blacked out. Some of my friends at the time would fill in the blanks about the events that took place on a particular night. They told me how I had driven them all over town and ended up at a tattoo shop and even gotten a tattoo. I still have it on my arm. It is a cross. Thank God. They also told me we got pulled over by the police and had our car searched. The police found enough loose random weed on the floorboard to scrape together and make a pile. They ended up letting us go. Thank God again. To this day I don't remember anything from that night.

I briefly had a relationship with a girl who worked in the pharmacy with me, and when that went south, so did the job. I would have lost the job before long anyway. The way it was going, I easily could have been charged with some very serious crimes.

Around that time, I met a guy we'll call Chuck. He was my dad's age. I met him because I was his drug dealer. I didn't get along with my own dad because of the choices I was making, and Chuck quickly became a father figure to me. Obviously, anyone in this lifestyle is not doing right and likely is not a good example, but in comparison to some of the other characters I knew and associated with, he was what I would consider a good old boy. He was an electrician at a major airport. He always tried to give me good advice, and I respected him and looked up to him. I think I even subconsciously came to believe that a person could do drugs all their life and still succeed as long as they controlled their addiction. He had a house and a wife, he paid his bills, and he went to work every day. It was a dangerous thing to believe.

One day I went by his house, and his daughter, whom we will call Tara, was there. She had moved from Oklahoma to stay with him permanently. She was the same age as me, and we quickly hit it off. Before you knew it, we were engaged. Next thing you know, I was living there too. I knew what I should do, and I did my very best to do it. Chuck put in a good word for me at the airline, and I put in the work on my end. I cleaned up long enough to go through an extensive interview process, went through twelve weeks of training eight hours a day on the computer system they used, and landed a job as a ticket agent. I was eighteen years old. It was my last decent accomplishment for a very long time.

Once I got the job, my new fiancée, Tara, and I moved into our first apartment together. It was the first time I had ever had anything in my name. Her uncle sold us a 1987 Cadillac Eldorado. It was in pristine condition. Everything was going great. Then we started doing meth again. This time, I had a new connection with an entirely different group of people. It was very different than anything I had done before. Our new start together turned into a nightmare as fast as it had started. We were spending all our money on dope. We were staying up four to seven days at a time. I was missing work more than I was there. We had all kinds of random people staying with us, including some girl who never left our couch. One night, some guy got stabbed in the leg in our living room. I don't know how I managed to keep my job as long as I did, but after about six months they fired me for attendance. I walked out of the airport, went to the airline credit union, and borrowed around four thousand dollars. I took the money with no intention of ever returning it. I went home and told Tara that I had good news and bad news. The bad news was that I had gotten fired. The good news was that I had four thousand dollars to party with. That's exactly what we did.

Within a month, we were completely spun out. We had both lost a considerable amount of weight, which was new to me. Our families knew at this point that things weren't good. Of course, her dad was still doing drugs with us. Things went downhill fast from here. The Cadillac overheated on the highway and blew a head gasket, which I had no money to fix. It was close to Christmastime, and her family wanted her to come back to Oklahoma for a couple weeks for the holidays. She wanted me to come too, of course. I told her I didn't want to go because of how bad I looked. I looked like walking death. I was close to six feet tall, but I was down to about 140 pounds. My normal weight was around 190 pounds at the time. I remember how upset she was and how much she cried. We got into a huge fight the day before she left, and I could see it in her eyes. I knew something was different. This was not the life she wanted. Even though she was doing the drugs with me, she didn't want to be. I know now she was hoping I would be her knight in shining armor and rescue her from this lifestyle. I was nowhere near a knight in shining armor. Neither one of us knew how much deeper down the rabbit hole I would end up going.

She left for Oklahoma the next day. One week later, she called me crying and told me she cheated on me with her ex-boyfriend. I was absolutely devastated. It was the first time my heart had ever been broken, and it hurt badly. So I did what I knew—more drugs. A lot more drugs. I lost everything. My job, my car, my apartment, and my fiancée. She made a decision to stay with her mom in Oklahoma and not come back. I was still good friends with her dad, and I moved back in with him. I began selling more and more to support my habit, and that meant meth was always around. Every day. All day. All night. I hardly ever charged Chuck for anything, since I was living there for free. Unfortunately, the drugs took a toll on his life as well. It wasn't long before his wife left him, and he was struggling at his job too.

Tara came back about a month later to visit him. Looking back, I know now that she was giving me a chance and hoping I would choose her over the drugs. Her dad and I were doing drugs in the garage all night. She didn't do any at all. She went to bed around 9 p.m. and asked if I was coming to bed. I told her I would be there in a minute. Hours later, she came out and asked one more time, and I told her the same, "I'll be there in a minute." Before I knew it, the sun was coming up, and I quickly went inside and slipped into bed with her. Unfortunately, she was like a statue. She wanted nothing to do with me, and I knew I had blown any chance to repair the relationship. She left the next day, and that was that.

From that moment on, I just didn't care about the consequences anymore. I didn't care what anyone tried to tell me. I was going to do what I was going to do.

Everyone else knew how bad I was getting. Even my original drug buddies, whom I had been running with for years, stopped hanging out with me. I watched as all my family and all my friends distanced themselves from me. That left only the worst of the worst addicts to run with.

# CHAPTER 7

# FIRST REHAB

I t wasn't long before I ended up broke, and for the first time ever, I didn't have a place to stay. I agreed to go to a thirty-day rehab program so I could then stay at my parents' house again and try to get back on my feet. My parents had high hopes that this would work. By the end of the thirty days, I even thought it was working. I felt great! I had gained some weight back, and I looked and felt pretty good. Unfortunately, it didn't last. I was right back to doing meth within days of being out of rehab. Of course, my parents didn't know that yet. I got some other job and ended up with a car again. I had started mowing lawns around the neighborhood for extra cash. At the time, my parents were just happy I was motivated and doing something. However, I was spending everything I made on meth. I didn't see it yet, but I was just a meth addict going around mowing lawns for money to do meth.

My addiction got worse and worse. Around this time, I ended up using needles for the first time. In terms of how addicted a person can become, this sealed the deal for me. Everyone has an image of what their "rock bottom" in life looks like or how it could look like, based on what they have experienced up to that point. The image I had of my own "rock bottom" was nowhere near what it would become. Using needles was like being thrown into a black hole and falling deeper and deeper into darkness. I lost all of my morals and inhibitions one by one. Nothing was off limits. No matter how wrong. No matter how sinful. No matter whom it hurt. So much for rehab.

## CHAPTER 8

# COOKING METH

In the meantime, I had plenty going on. I was mowing the lawn for some of my parents' neighbors, Avery and Chasity, who lived across the street. They were also meth addicts. Even more, they had a meth cook, whom we will call Brandon, as one of their suppliers. I knew who he was, but you don't just walk up to a meth cook and say, "Hey, I heard you cook meth. Can I get some?" But it just so happened that he needed his lawn mown at his house. I was mowing Avery's lawn while he was there, and he stopped me and asked if I could mow his lawn too. With zero hesitation, I blurted out, "Sure!" We loaded the mower in his car right then and there, and I rode with him to his house.

When we got there, we pulled into a long driveway and parked about twenty feet from the garage door. I had no idea what was about to happen. He walked up to the garage door and manually opened it. I couldn't believe it. Inside were three people running around back and forth to different stations all over the garage. There were beakers and flasks and hoses everywhere. It was a fully functional meth lab. I'm not sure if he ever really intended for me to mow his lawn. I'm pretty sure I only mowed that one time. He closed the garage door once we were inside. We walked through the garage and into the kitchen. All the counters were full of various glass jars and trays. The fridge and freezer were full of jars and dishes that also had meth in them. There were so many dishes everywhere, but there was no food anywhere in the house. Every dish was being used for cooking meth. After I mowed the lawn, he drove me back to my parents' house and dropped me off. He had given me a very big bag of meth that turned out to be far stronger than any I had ever done before. It was fresh and pure.

A few days later, he called me and asked if I knew anyone who could get some red phosphorus. I didn't even know what that was, but it just so happened that a girl I knew had called me the day before and asked me if I knew anyone that needed that exact thing. Her boyfriend, who was also an acquaintance of mine, went to jail, and she was left trying to get rid of it. I told Brandon that I might know someone. I gave her a call, and one thing led to another. It wasn't long before I became friends with Brandon. This is when things really got crazy. From that day on, I was there every day. I officially moved in. He started teaching me everything. Before I knew it, I was spun out in a whole new way. I thought I was on top of the world. I was selling larger amounts than ever before. I thought I was really something because I was cooking meth.

Meanwhile, as I got in deeper and deeper, something else new happened. I was on the lookout for the feds. I had never been paranoid before, but now I was doing things that could get me real time. I was also in the spotlight now. Meth cooks are the ones whom the police are actively looking for. For the kind of meth we were cooking, we needed three main ingredients. The police call them precursors. One of the precursors was pseudoephedrine. Back then, there were no laws limiting how many boxes of pills containing pseudoephedrine someone could buy at one time. We would drive about an hour and a half away and start a route back hitting every store we could. We would buy every box they had on the shelf at every store. We did this every week. We also had to get a few federally monitored items at feed stores. I quickly noticed that when we would buy the pills and other ingredients we needed, the people who worked in the stores would look at us strangely. It was like they knew what we were doing. Then I started to notice we were being followed most of the time. I would see the same group of people all day and all hours of the night, but in all different cars. My paranoia was getting worse.

One night, at 2 or 3 a.m., we were desperate for some supplies. We went into a twenty-four-hour grocery store and bought a variety of things that we normally knew better than to buy all together. We were pretty much the only customers in the store. Our hands were stained yellow from iodine, and our clothes smelled like a meth lab all the time. We were almost done checking out when suddenly, a police officer came over and started taking items out of the bags and placing them on the counter. He was furious. Every time he set an item on the counter, he would say, "This can be used to cook meth," "This can be used to cook meth." Oh no! Like I said, we knew not to buy certain items all together, but we were desperate. When those items were rung up together, it set off a red flag. I had no idea what to do. Brandon told me to just start walking to the car. We did. The police officer followed us on foot and got the license plate number. They didn't have enough evidence to arrest us or they would have, but it wasn't a good situation. We knew things were starting to get bad, so we did what any meth addict would do. We proceeded to a few more stores, got what we needed, and went back to the lab and cooked more meth as if nothing had happened.

CHAPTER 9

# THE TRAIN

I don't know why I allowed my life to become what it did. Nowhere to go. No one to call. No help. No way out. Every day was spent living in fear, looking over my shoulder. No rest. No peace.

I had just finished helping my friend cook some more meth. He had already left the house. I was getting too paranoid to stay there any longer. I didn't have a car at that moment, so I took off walking.

My life was like that. One minute I had a car, and the next I didn't. I went through at least twelve cars in a twenty-year period. I would pay a few hundred dollars for a cheap car or even trade some dope for one. I would never get it inspected or insured or even registered. I would get pulled over and get multiple tickets for it and then never pay them. The tickets would turn into warrants, and then the next time I got pulled over, the police would arrest me and take me to jail and impound the car. I would sit out the warrants, get out of jail with no money, and lose the car. This happened over and over and over. Crazy, right? I recall the saying, "If you always do what you have always done, you will always get what you have always gotten."

That day, I took off walking from Brandon's house. My pockets were completely full of meth. I had a cell phone, but it wasn't connected at the moment, so I headed toward the nearest pay phone. This was back when they still had pay phones at most gas stations. I was getting more and more paranoid with every second and with each passing car. I knew there was a chance that I was being investigated by the DEA by this time. The paranoia took over.

I couldn't stand it anymore. I had to get off the street. There were some woods on my right with a trail going into them. I knew that there was a store somewhere in that direction on the next street over. There was a trailer park right there as well, and I figured the people who lived there had worn a path from walking back and forth to the store.

I quickly headed down the trail, into the woods, and out of sight. After walking for what seemed like forever, I realized I was no longer on any trail. I was trudging through thick thorns and briars and getting cut up. I thought about turning back. I looked back and saw thorns behind me as far as I could see. Just then, I saw a train not too far in front of me, going really slow. Perfect! I could just jump on and take a short slow ride out of the woods. I jumped on and climbed up the ladder a few steps. Before I knew it, the train had sped up significantly. I continued up the ladder until I was on top of one of the boxcars. I was just going to wait until it stopped. We went through a town without stopping. Then another town. Then a third. I realized I had to get off this train before I got any further away. I came up with a great plan. I would wait until the next town and jump off so I could be near a phone. I would climb down the ladder as low to the ground as I could get, facing the direction the train was moving.

There I was, hanging off the side of a train that was clearly going at least sixty miles per hour. I held my breath, and I'm pretty sure I said a prayer that went something like, "God, please don't let me die." Then I jumped as far as I could away from the train. My plan was to land on my feet and start running when I hit the ground. I was obviously high. I jumped. I did land on my feet, but when I did, the momentum threw me to the ground with an insane amount of force. I landed on the left side of my head and started sliding with the train and toward the train. My eyes were somehow stuck wide open. I could see myself getting closer to the train, and I was starting to think I was going to get run over. I'm sure that it all happened in just a matter of seconds, but it felt like an eternity. In my head, it was happening in slow motion for sure. Thank God, I finally stopped sliding before I got to the train. I lay on the ground until the train passed. I tried to stand up and then fell back down. I stood up again and felt very thick blood oozing down my head. In fact, I was covered in blood. I had on a white t-shirt and a black-and-white flannel jacket. Both were splattered in red. I looked like I had been hit by a bus. Or like I had just jumped off a train.

My first thought probably should have been, "Am I okay?" But it wasn't. It was, "Do I still have the dope in my pockets?" I did. Whew. I was worried. I stumbled my way through whatever small town I had made it to, walked into a gas station, and asked if I could use their phone. I told them I had wrecked a dirt bike so they weren't suspicious. I'm sure by the way I looked they didn't buy it. I called up a buddy, and they drove all the way to come get me for just a little dope, and then they took me where I asked to go. When I got there, I fell asleep in a chair and woke up two days later with a pounding headache. This is just one of many examples of how I know that God was protecting me, even when I was making so many horrible choices. There is no way I would be alive after this incident without God.

# CHAPTER 10

# MY MOM'S ATTIC

My life was crazy at this time. I was not allowed at my parents' house at this point. However, I always seemed to find a way to break in while they were at work. I would eat their food, steal whatever I needed from them, and do meth there. One day while I was there, I heard a knock at the door. I had been awake a very long time, and I was so high and paranoid. I thought it was the cops, so I ran into the hallway, pulled the attic door down from the ceiling, climbed up, and closed the door behind me. Hours went by.

"Cory? Cory? Cory!!!" I heard my mom's voice calling my name. She sounded like she was at the end of a long tunnel. I opened my eyes, and there was my mom, with a look of sadness, heartbreak, and terror that I will never forget. She was standing at the top of the ladder leading up to the attic, looking at me lying on her attic floor. I could hear the anguish in her voice too. I wasn't even supposed to be there, and she had come home to find me passed out in her attic. I had absolutely no explanation to offer. Those looks became the norm for all my family. My dad, my mom, my sister, and anyone else who loved me all had the same look on their face every time they saw me. They were completely heartbroken. There was nothing they could do. My parents watched year after year after year as their only son slipped farther and farther away. I was almost unrecognizable. I was an addict and a thief. I was lost and hopeless.

# CHAPTER 11

# POLICE HELICOPTERS

A round this time, Brandon and I both decided that things were getting a bit too hot and that we should start cooking at a new location. I moved in with a girl I knew—we will call Valerie— and we started cooking there for a brief time.

One day, I had just made a call setting up a deal to go get some more red phosphorus. Valerie lived in a neighborhood that had just one way in and out. There was a four-way stop sign that you had to go through to get out of the neighborhood. We jumped in her Mustang and took off. I was driving. We were coming up to that four-way stop, and I noticed a man who looked out of place walking down the sidewalk toward us. About the time I saw him, he put his hand to his mouth and then quickly back down again. Just as I started to process the thought that he could be an undercover agent, I had to slam on the breaks. There were police cars coming from every direction! By the time the car stopped, there was an officer coming directly toward me on foot with his gun pulled and pointed at me.

I knew what was coming. I quickly threw off my seat belt so I didn't get tangled in it. By the time I got it off, he was dragging me out of the car. He threw me on the ground and searched me. I had a joint in my small pocket that he didn't find. He cuffed me and threw me in the back of a police car. I could hear a helicopter hovering above. I slid the joint down into the seat of the police car. As I watched them pull Valerie out of the car and search first her and then her purse, all I could think of was the meth lab I had in her garage a block away. The officers pulled a meth pipe full of meth out of Valerie's purse. They were waving it around so I could see it too. They pulled her off to the side. Then they came and got me out of the squad car and walked me over to our car. They put the meth pipe they had found in her purse in front of me and asked if it was mine. I said no, of course. Then, unexpectedly, they removed the cuffs from me. They told us they had made a mistake and that they were looking for two African American males who robbed a gas station up the street. I was a white male and she was a white female. I couldn't believe it, but they let us go. So we did what any meth addict would do: we got back in the car and went to make the deal we were headed to make in the first place.

These kinds of events began to happen regularly. It was absolutely crazy. We did decide, however, that we should find another place to cook.

CHAPTER 12

# METH LAB ON FIRE

After a while, Brandon started cooking meth at the house of my parents' neighbors across the street—Avery and Chasity. Mowing their lawn was how I met Brandon in the first place. We started cooking there in the backyard in a shed. The whole backyard was like a junkyard. There were old cars and trucks and junk everywhere. You could barely walk back there, and you had to stay on the trails between everything. We would come and cook when we needed to and then leave and go back to Brandon's.

One night, we were on our way over to Avery's to finish cooking. I will never forget how it happened. It was around dusk, just a couple minutes from getting dark. The sky had radiant oranges and reds in it. We exited off the highway and turned right. They lived in a corner house at the third stop sign from the highway. By the time we had gotten to the second stop sign, the sun had set and it was dark. Suddenly, we heard sirens coming from multiple directions. Then we saw flashing lights between the houses up and down the street of the house where we were cooking. We inched a little closer. Now we could see fire trucks, police cars, and hazmat trucks parked all around the house. There were guys in full hazmat suits carrying our jars out of the house. It was like a scene from a movie, but much worse. My heart was racing. This was not good.

I shouted, "Turn around now!" We had to go back to Brandon's house and clear it out. Even though we were doing most of the cooking at the house of my parents' neighbors, we still had plenty of meth and precursors to cook meth at Brandon's. Avery and Chasity knew the consequences of what would happen if the house ever got raided. However, we also knew there was a pretty good chance that if anything ever did happen, they could end up giving our names to get a lesser sentence. We hurried back to Brandon's and loaded up the car with everything we had, and then I drove it to Chuck's. I moved around every few days after this.

Brandon and his girlfriend continued to stay at his house. Because my parents lived across the street from the house where we had the lab, I would ask my mom what was happening every chance I got over the next few weeks. It turned out that an extension cord caught on fire in the backyard, and when the fire department came, they found the lab. Chasity got arrested immediately for manufacturing methamphetamine. Avery ran on foot and was found a few hours later. He was also arrested for manufacturing methamphetamine. During the entire incident, their young kids were standing outside in the cold. My mom took a blanket across the street and covered them up while the scene unfolded. The kids were taken into CPS custody. Chasity got out relatively quickly. A few years later, I heard that Avery died in prison.

Unfortunately, this incident was not over by any means. Within a few weeks, two more big meth labs got busted in the same neighborhood. That meant only one thing: people were talking. I was running scared. However, Brandon was casual and unconcerned as usual.

At some point, I started staying with another friend, Chelsea, who was also Avery's ex-wife, and she ended up being his power of attorney. She was intimately involved in the case as it unfolded. A point came when she told me that names had been given and federal indictments were going out soon. I called Brandon and told him he needed to chill out and get anything he had out of his house. I got rid of everything and stopped cooking. He didn't. A few weeks later, the feds showed up at his door with a federal indictment and arrested him for manufacturing methamphetamine. No one knew where I was staying at the time, not even Brandon.

A week after he was arrested by the feds, while I was sleeping early in the morning, Chelsea woke me up in a panic like she had seen a ghost. She said, "You are never going to believe who is here!" I got up and walked to the front door. I opened it, and standing in front of me was Brandon. His car was parked out front. My heart sank. I thought for sure the feds were right around the corner. He told me he was out temporarily on bond. He also told me the feds were the nicest people he ever talked to. The last thing he told me was that the feds had told him that they were going to send special teams from all over the United States to take down meth cooks and dealers in the metroplex. Then he left. He came all the way to tell me that. I don't even know how he knew where I was.

I know that my name was mentioned in the case because DEA agents showed up at my parents' door looking for me. To this day, I have no idea why I was not indicted as well. I believe that once again God was looking out for me, even in the midst of my addiction. We will get much more into that soon enough.

## CHAPTER 13

# FEDS, FEDS, FEDS

D ay and night, I was constantly paranoid. I was still selling but not cooking. I would set up a meeting point with someone I was selling to and change it three times on the way to throw off the chances of being set up. I would even cancel the sale at the last minute. I was extremely suspicious of everyone, even people I had known for years. I couldn't trust anyone. I knew there were warrants for my arrest; I had no car registration or insurance and no valid license. I would get pulled over, and then someone on the other end of the radio would tell the officer to let me go. I assume I had a DNT on me: "Do Not Detain." This happened over and over.

One time, I was leaving my dealer's house with a lot of meth. I had it taped up under the dash. Immediately, I got pulled over by an officer who was waiting down the street. He frantically searched my pockets, found nothing, cuffed me, and threw me in the back of the police car. There were two passengers with me, and he had them wait outside my car while he searched it. He could easily have found the drugs, but then I heard another officer come on the radio and tell him to let me go. When he heard he had to let me go, he was furious. He grabbed me out of the car and searched me again. Then he uncuffed me and pushed me toward my car and told me to get lost.

So many crazy things like this happened. At this point, I believe that it was more important to whoever was investigating that I was out making deals instead of being locked up. I don't even think it was me they wanted; it was the people I was associating with.

It is terrible what this drug can do to a person. The effects that methamphetamine and other drugs can have on a person's mind, will, and emotions can only be truly repaired by God. There is a slow rewiring that takes place when a person does meth on a continuous, long-term basis. Their perception of reality begins to change, and ultimately they will have a very difficult time distinguishing what is real and what is not. I knew throughout the years of using meth that this was happening to me, and I certainly realized the signs. It was a very scary place to be. Even if a person does successfully get clean, these effects do not automatically go away. I didn't even know just how much repair would be needed until years after I got clean. Even now, I am still in recovery, working with God, and being restored.

# CHAPTER 14

# OKLAHOMA AND BIG CHIEF

Sometime soon after this, I found out that Chuck was moving to Oklahoma. I was looking for a fresh start. What better place to do that than the place where Tara was? Chuck decided to let me move to Oklahoma with him to get a new start. I had nothing but good intentions. I wanted to straighten up. I made a commitment to Chuck and myself: no more meth. We just drank here and there instead. I basically only slept and ate the first couple weeks. I met one of the neighbors in the apartment complex; we will call him John. Around the third week of being in Oklahoma, I borrowed John's car and drove a block away to get some beer. I got back to John's apartment and went in and shut the door behind me.

He had sliding glass doors, and you could see through the blinds out to the parking lot where his car was parked. About fifteen minutes after I had gotten back, three police cars pulled up. They got out and walked toward the breezeway where John's door was. I remember thinking, "Surely not." There was a loud knock at the door. Since I had no drugs on me and wasn't even doing meth, and I hadn't done anything wrong since coming to Oklahoma, I opened the door. It was a sergeant and two other officers. He was holding a clipboard in his hand. He said he was there to write me a ticket for running a stop sign in the grocery store parking lot fifteen minutes earlier.

In disbelief of what was happening, I signed the ticket, handed back the clipboard, opened the door, and waved them out. I closed the door. The next thing I knew, they were all out in the parking lot, searching the car! I opened the door, took one step out, and said, "Hey, what are you doing?" The sergeant pulled his gun out and started walking toward me. He grabbed me and threw me on the stairs, ripping my shirt and jeans in the process. He told me I was under arrest for public intoxication. He then searched me and found only cigarette rolling papers. I ended up getting charged with possession of drug paraphernalia in addition to the public intoxication. I spent almost a year in the city jail for those two things.

While in city jail, I was sleeping on a bench one day when I heard a voice say, "Get up." Without opening my eyes, I said, "F#*% you!" The next thing I knew, I was being picked up by one of the biggest guys I have ever seen. He was an American Indian man named Big Chief. My feet were literally dangling in the air. Before I could get a word out, he headbutted me in my nose and then dropped me. I slunk to the ground and lay there and bled. My nose would not stop bleeding for a long time. It eventually did, but my nose has been slightly crooked ever since.

This was not the fresh start I had envisioned. The day I finally got out, they took me to court before releasing me, and the judge gave me six months of probation for running the stop sign. I had come here to get out of trouble and maybe even reconcile with Tara, but I got off to a bad start. Once I was out of jail, I went to see Chuck. Tara was living with him now. She was also neck-deep back into meth. She wanted absolutely nothing to do with me. I decided it was time to leave. I came to Oklahoma on vacation and left on probation.

**CHAPTER 15**

# NEW ROCK BOTTOM

I came back to Texas, and since I had been in jail for a year, I was clean and looked the best I had in years. My parents decided to let me move back in with them. Unfortunately, because I was back in my old stomping grounds, it didn't take long to get right back on meth. My situation and health quickly deteriorated again, and of course my parents kicked me out again. I didn't have the connections I had before, since everyone I had known was in prison. I had no money and nowhere to go. I was getting meth from whoever I could by stealing whatever I could and pawning it. I got so bad that I was putting needles in my arms multiple times a day. Once I counted thirteen times in one day.

Things were worse than ever. No one would help me, and I was alone. I wanted to quit so badly, but I could not. I hated what I was doing, and I hated myself. I would get so mad and throw all my needles in a ditch somewhere, and then the next day I would go back and get them and use them again. I shared needles with all kinds of people, including someone who had officially been diagnosed with AIDS. I even used random needles I would find on the ground if I needed one badly enough.

I was always hungry and always tired. I had no place to live, no car, and no help. My weight was down to about 135 pounds. I slept wherever

I could, under bridges, in the bleachers at schools, and sometimes in my parents' backyard in my dad's boat. Sometimes my mom would find me early in the morning when she was watering flowers in her garden. The dogs would give me away. My dad had told her that under no circumstances was I to be on the property, ever. No helping me in any way. However, my mom never gave up on her baby boy. With that same look of heartbreak and utter sadness, she would hand me some food and tell me I couldn't be there. My parents assumed they would get a phone call someday letting them know I had been found dead somewhere.

CHAPTER 16

# SAVED AT LAST

One day, it was pouring down rain and I was walking down the street near my parents' house. I was so tired and worn out. I had tried going to rehab and every other solution everyone recommended to me. My dad used to say I just didn't have enough will-power. Nothing ever worked. I fell on my knees in the middle of the street in the pouring rain and asked God, "If You are real, please help me." I got up and walked toward my parents' house. My dad was at work during the day. I knocked on the door, and my mom answered. I was soaking wet and crying. I told her I wanted to try going to church. She had already started going to a church with a friend. She, like me, was willing to try anything. She told me to be at her house early Sunday morning, so I came.

I know without a doubt it was absolutely the exact church I was supposed to be in at the time. God knew what He was doing. He always does. It was a tiny little church with a congregation of maybe thirty people total. That was good for me because I looked like death and was embarrassed. The fewer people who saw me, the better. It was not like I had imagined. Everyone was in casual everyday clothes, and they all seemed happy. They a had a joy that I could only dream of. I don't even know when was the last time I had smiled.

When I saw the preacher, I was surprised again. He had a shaved head and goatee and was also dressed casually. He preached a message that spoke directly to me. I knew that God was tugging at my heart. Up until this point I had considered anyone who went to church to be tree-huggers. My experience at this church proved me wrong. There was a couple there that day who treated me with kindness from the second they met me. They asked me what my story was, and when I told them, they took me in that day. They took me to their home in the middle of nowhere and helped me clean up. They set me up in a three-day program they said would help.

This program took place at a hotel, and we stayed on-site the whole three days. There were about one hundred of us there. We each had one roommate, guys with guys and girls with girls. I won't go into exact detail about how the program worked, but I ended up lying on the ground, face down in front of everyone, screaming and crying as loud as I could, begging Jesus to come into my heart and save me. He did save me that day. From that moment, I knew in my heart I was different.

After I got up off the ground, one of the facilitators came up to me and waved a white towel an inch from my face. He told me that this is where my addiction would be from now on. I didn't know exactly what he meant by that yet. A few minutes later, we were done for the day, and I went up to my room.

I noticed that my roommate hadn't shown up for the last segment. When I opened the door of my hotel room, a huge cloud of meth smoke came pouring out. There were multiple people in the room, all smoking meth. I couldn't believe it. Just like the towel, it was in my face that fast. I turned around and walked away. It was the first time I had ever said no to meth. I didn't turn him in. However, I definitely couldn't stay in that room. Instead, I went and knocked on a girl's door whom I had met there. I told her what had happened, and she said I could stay there for the night.

I felt great. My mind was clear, and I was smiling. I had forgotten what it felt like to have a clear mind and to feel good. One thing led to another, and we ended up sleeping together. What happened afterward was the strange part. I felt guilty and ashamed because we weren't married. Once I gave my life to Jesus, certain things weren't the same ever again. I had a sensitivity to sin. I felt convicted when I did wrong. I knew something was different in my heart.

When the program was over, I came out feeling on top of the world! My mom picked me up, took one look at me, and started crying. I was happy and smiling. She hadn't seen me smile in years. I told her everything that had happened. I was never going to do meth again! I was never even going to sin again. I was a new man. I was going to find out who Jesus was and be all about Jesus. I was going to go to church every Sunday and get my life together.

Two weeks later, I relapsed and did meth again. For the first time in my life, I felt convicted for doing meth. I felt the Spirit inside me grieve for the first time. I knew I was different, but I had already messed up. It was off to the races again.

# CHAPTER 17

# HOMELESS IN
# THE WOODS

I would like to say that I only messed up a few times and then got myself together and lived happily ever after, but that's not what happened at all. I spent the next ten years in and out of jail, in and out of very toxic relationships, and ultimately homeless again. During one particular time I ended up homeless, I had been living in motels all around the metroplex, and things just weren't working out. I ran out of money and dope and had no other resources. I had no car and no place to live. At my final checkout time, I left the motel on foot with a dog I had acquired while staying there. His name was (and still is) Jack, as in Jack the Ripper. He is a small black-and-brown rat terrier. He is old and a bit whiny now, so everyone calls him Jack the Yipper.

Jack and I left the motel on foot and started walking. It was winter and freezing cold. Before long, we came to a large grocery store on our right and a large wooded area on our left. We walked up to the store. I left Jack tied up outside and went in. I grabbed a shopping cart and started going through the store, throwing into the cart anything and everything I could think of in order to survive in the woods across the street. I grabbed a tent, a machete, a cooler, a propane tent heater, blankets, and lots of cans of nonperishable food. The cart was completely full.

I had no money to pay for any of these things, and I had to think of something quick. There were always workers standing at the exits and checking receipts. How was I going to get this shopping cart full of items I was planning on stealing past those workers without a receipt? I pulled out my phone and put it to my ear. I started acting like I was very mad at whoever I was talking to. I was loudly pretending to curse them out and make threats. While I was yelling and cursing at the person everyone thought I was on the phone with, I just walked right by the checkout and then right by the people checking receipts! I was acting so irate that they were afraid to confront me and ask for a receipt. It worked! I grabbed my dog, and we walked straight across the parking lot and then across the street.

I pushed that shopping cart right into the woods. I took out the machete and started clearing a path. Once I was deep into the woods, I cleared a spot big enough for a tent and some extra space for a fire. I got everything set up, and then I was exhausted. I was coming down from the meth now and had no way of getting more. I walked back across the street, went back in the store, and stole a shopping cart full of beer. "This will get me through until I figure something out," I thought.

Did I mention it was cold? Well, it got colder. A lot colder. It started snowing that night. My propane tent heater only lasted four hours before running out of fuel. After that, it was ice cold. My poor dog couldn't stop shivering. We both were living on spam, potted meat, and canned soup. Weeks went by, and it kept getting colder. It was a cold most people don't understand. It wasn't like going from your house to your car and then from your car to the store and then back to the car and then the house again. It's staying outside and never getting warm until your bones are cold all the way through. I remember my parents came out to the woods where I was staying once and took me to take a shower and warm up.

It took me hours to actually get warm. Even on the coldest setting, the shower felt hot. When I was warm and fed, they took me back to the woods and dropped me off. I hope I never have to know the pain they must have felt watching my life unfold the way it did. They were worrying day and night, never knowing if I was all right or even alive. They once told me they felt the most peace when I was in jail because at least they knew where I was and that I was alive.

At some point, I ended up with a bicycle. I knew I had to do something. I started getting up early every morning to look for a job, any job. I would ride the bike to the nearby fast-food place and go into the bathroom and shave with my stolen razors and shaving cream and clean up a bit. Everything I had was stolen. Afterward, I would ride around, putting in applications at every place I could. I looked like walking death, and it was hard to get a job. My phone was disconnected by this time, so unless I got hired on the spot, it wasn't going to work. No employer could even call me to let me know they were hiring me.

Finally, I did get hired at a discount store as a stocker. They hired me on at $6.75 per hour, and I worked three two-hour days. That was six hours per week total. Obviously, this wasn't going to work forever, but it was something. On my first day of work, a man was there who normally worked at a different location but was filling in. Somehow, we got to talking about my situation. He handed me a business card and told me to call the number on the card and tell the person on the other end about my situation. After work, that's what I did. A woman answered. I told her about my situation, and she told me to start packing. She asked me for directions to the woods, and then she came and picked me up.

I stayed at her house that night and got to take a warm shower and eat warm food for the first time in a long time. The next day, she took me to meet a friend of hers. She told him about my situation, and he put me in a duplex that night that already had electricity and water. I knew God had worked this out for me. God has always done things like this my whole life. He has an amazing way of winning someone over by showing them His love and grace.

I was given chance after chance after chance. I wanted to make this work—I really did. Unfortunately, my job was now a ten-mile ride to and from work. Ten miles just to work two hours and then ride back. I was able to make that work for about three weeks. After that, I quit. You can guess what happened next. I took whatever money I had made and put it toward dope. The cycle started all over again. I eventually got kicked out and was running the streets again. Over and over and over it went. I say again, if you always do what you've always done, you will always get what you've always gotten.

CHAPTER 18

# EIGHTEEN- MONTH REHAB

Ever since I was saved, doing drugs made me miserable. That's part of how I knew I was different. My heart had changed. The fun had been taken out of it. I felt like I was disappointing God, and I hated it. But I could not stop. I knew now that God was the only thing that had even shown any evidence of working. I decided I would try a long-term Christian rehab. I thought to myself, "I just need more clean time and more God." I got accepted to an eighteen-month program. My parents were happy to help drive me there.

The rehab program was in the middle of nowhere, way outside of the city on some acreage. They had an arrangement worked out with a Christian resort. There were hotels on-site, a large conference building, an on-site restaurant, and a lake. There were about twenty cabins on-site as well. Each cabin could accommodate about twenty guys. The guys in the rehab would essentially work to pay for room and board and food. We would work eight-hour days three days per week, and the other two days we would spend in eight hours of Bible study with various pastors and teachers. The work would vary depending on what the resort needed. You might be helping with hotel housekeeping, lake maintenance, groundskeeping, kitchen staff, or even helping build a water park.

I held multiple different positions while there. I started out on the lawn crew. I also helped clean septic tanks and waited tables. After about six months, I was asked to be an intern. That was essentially a promotion into a leadership position. The position came with my own room instead of a bunk bed with twenty other guys as well as some other freedoms. A new job came with it. I was put in charge of the kitchen crew that was responsible for preparing all of the meals for the hundred-plus guys who were in rehab with me. Breakfast, lunch, and dinner. There was a chef there who had trained in Spain who taught me how to do a few things. He made amazing cinnamon banana pancakes and jalapeno burgers. I had access to a very large commercial kitchen that was fully stocked to accommodate up to 1500 people who would come stay at the resort. A few other guys who were also in rehab worked for me. Of course, none of us were ever paid any money. All of the work we did was for room and board only. That alone was a very humbling experience.

I spent more time in the Bible and more time learning about God than at any other time in my life. God revealed Himself to me during my time there in some very amazing ways. One night, we all piled into a bunch of vans, and the leaders drove us to a Christian college to hear some guest speakers from South America, a husband and wife. The event was in a huge auditorium with stadium seating. Our group, guys who were all in rehab, was sitting up in the balcony. Now, I believed in Jesus and that He died for our sins and that we are saved by grace. I believed that God works in our lives and speaks to us. I did not, however, believe in any of that phony-baloney stuff like falling on the floor. However, that is exactly what started happening right in front of my eyes.

At the end of the service, the speakers said, "If you want to be touched by God, come up to the stage." A long line formed. Each person would go up to the stage, and either the husband or the wife would walk up to them. Then they would either pray or say something, and the person would fall on the ground. I remember thinking, "Nope. No way." "How much are these people getting paid to fall down on stage?" I wondered. Then I began to tell all the guys around me what I thought about it. I was so sure it was fake that I decided I would prove it. I told all my fellow rehabbers I was going to go down there and intentionally not fall, no matter what. I was going to stand my ground to prove once and for all how ridiculous this nonsense was.

I walked right down there and got in line. Finally, it was my turn. I walked up the steps and onto the stage. The wife came over to me. She was a very small lady, and I'm sure I was thinking how that would make this even easier. I was a pretty big guy, and there was no way she was pushing me down onto the floor. She walked up to me and didn't say anything. She just very lightly pushed on my chest with the tips of her fingers two times. I didn't budge. I had one leg behind me in a braced stance position. I wasn't going down. Then, after that second little push, she just smiled at me with this slight grin and turned her hand with her palm up like she was going to blow a kiss, and she blew across her hand toward me.

The next thing I remember, my eyes were closed tightly, and I was falling. The next thing I remember after that was feeling myself on the ground in a fetal position with my fists, my teeth, and my eyes clenched extremely hard. I tried to get up, but I could not. It felt like I was stuck to the floor. Every part of my body was pressed to the floor. I couldn't move or open my eyes. I had no concept of time, so I don't know how long it was before my eyes opened, but they finally did. I realized I was still lying on my side, facing away from the audience. I started to try to get up, and I immediately fell back down. After a minute or so I tried again. This time I was successful. When I stood up, I felt like I was coming out of a dream world. I quickly made my way to a bench on the stage only a few feet away. I sat there another minute or so, and then I looked up toward the audience. My goodness, there were still over a thousand people watching the whole thing!

I got very uncomfortable very fast. I wanted to escape from being in front of all those people as fast as possible. I stood up and started walking off stage. I had an indescribable and amazing feeling running through my body, like electricity, intensifying with every step I took! I started smiling uncontrollably. It was a feeling of warmth and love. I didn't stop smiling and feeling this way for three whole days. Looking back, I know with certainty that I was in God's presence that day. I am no Moses, but I am reminded of how Moses' countenance changed when he saw God's face. I did not see God's face, but I was changed that day.

Nothing I had ever experienced and nothing I have experienced to this day ever felt that good. It was the purest, warmest feeling I have ever felt. That experience for me brings a new understanding of "every knee should bow" (Philippians 2:10 ESV). When that time comes, whether a person wants to or not, everyone will fall to the floor in God's presence. No one can stand. If God says bow, we will bow. So now I absolutely do believe in all that phony-baloney stuff! There is nothing phony about it!

After this, I was on fire for God. Now my recovery would be forever solidified. How could I ever mess up again? Not long after this event, still in rehab, I was chosen to work on a small volunteer team and go help an older gentleman clean out his garage and house. Only the most trusted guys were picked for this. Yep, that was me, all right. Trustworthy. I think this was about six months into the rehab program. It was the longest I had ever been clean since starting drugs.

One day I was helping in his home, and I needed to use the restroom. He pointed me down the hall. I went into the bathroom and closed the door. The linen closet door was open. I glanced in that direction, and immediately my eye caught something very familiar. Syringes. A whole case of them. This guy was diabetic. Instantly, the feeling of shooting up came over me, and that was it. I put a ten-pack of syringes in my pocket, and by the end of the day I was gone. After everything that had happened and all that clean time, it was over. I was off to the races again.

I left the rehab, and I was shooting meth again by the end of the night. My life spiraled out of control faster than ever before, and it wasn't long before things were just like they had been. I had developed a deep relationship with God, and I know that His heart was breaking. My heart was breaking too. From this time on, I was so sad. An emptiness and sadness that no words can express came over me. I never want to experience that again. Maybe some of you are experiencing this yourself or even for someone you love. I pray right now that God allows you to feel His presence in this moment. I pray that He allows you to taste His goodness. God loves you and has a plan for you. His plans are for good and not evil. He is intimately involved in your life, even if you don't know it.

# CHAPTER 19

# CHRISTMAS EVE FIRE

Sometime later, my parents were away from home, and I needed a place to cook meth. Yep, I was back messing around with cooking meth again. Not much, but some. It was Christmas Eve. My parents were not home. I had nowhere to go. I wasn't allowed at my parents' house. I couldn't go to my sister's house. I had no real friends. I was alone. I broke into my parents' house. I could usually find where they had hidden spare keys around, and I would use those to go in. I was using their stove to extract ephedrine out of some pills. The pills were broken down and dissolved in a very flammable solvent, called methanol, in a Pyrex dish. My parents had a gas stove. I knew better than to do this using an open flame, but I was desperate. The methanol started to boil too much, so I grabbed a hot pad and tried to pick up the dish and get it off the stove. The hot pad caught on fire. Then the methanol did too. I had a bowl of liquid on fire in my hands. I dropped the bowl of fire on the linoleum floor, and it spread into a large puddle of fire, which then spread to some jackets hanging on a kitchen chair and then to the curtains, which also caught on fire. My mom and dad's kitchen was up in flames.

I had to make a choice fast. I could try to put out the fire on the floor or tackle the bigger fire on the chair with all the jackets hanging on it. I chose the chair. I grabbed the flaming chair, jackets and all, raced out to the backyard, and hosed it down. I kept thinking that one of the neighbors was going to see this and would call the police. I hurried back in, grabbed a pan, and started filling it up with water and throwing it on the fire as fast as I could. I finally did get it all put out, but the whole house was filled with thick smoke. I had to let the smoke out, but I was afraid the neighbors would see it and call the fire department. If the neighbors saw me there at all, they would call the police. I started opening multiple windows, just enough to start venting out the house.

Meanwhile, I started trying to clean up the damage. There was no hiding this. The whole linoleum kitchen floor was completely black and melted. Jackets were burned. The chair was burned. The curtains were burned. I did the best I could with the mess and decided I would wait for my parents to come home and tell them I was cooking green beans and somehow started a fire. Looking back, it is hard for me to believe that I was so messed up that I didn't even consider that you don't use grease when cooking green beans. I was completely out of my mind. When my parents came home, they were devastated. I was immediately thrown out of the house. I had anticipated this, and I had arranged for a ride. My ride showed up a few minutes later as I was walking down the street. I had him circle back around the block and park at the far back of my parents' property. I jumped the fence into their backyard and grabbed the various jars full of meth ingredients out of all the places where I had hidden them in their yard. I tossed everything in the trunk of my friend's car and hopped in with him, and we drove off.

This event is one of my biggest regrets from that time in my life. I had ruined Christmas in a way that would never be forgotten. My parents did not deserve any of this. I was sinking lower and lower into an abyss out of which most people never return. The depths of darkness that I reached are unspeakable. Tears are rolling down my cheek right now, just thinking of the pain and torment that I caused my family and that I felt myself, living out this absolute nightmare of a life.

# CHAPTER 20

# BUSTED

After close to another ten years of running from God, it finally happened. I had been up and down for years. Sometimes I had plenty of drugs and could stay with whomever I wanted, and sometimes I didn't. At this particular time, I was selling a fairly large amount on a daily basis. One day, I had just picked up a batch and was on my way back to where I was staying. I didn't drive much anymore since there were warrants out on me, and I figured out it was safer to have someone with no warrants drive me in a legal car. Either way, a cop ended up behind us and was following us for a while. I had a feeling we were going to get pulled over, and since I had warrants out for me and a bunch of dope on me, I was definitely going to jail if I got caught.

I had evaded the police many times on foot before. I would always run down into sewer tunnels and keep going until I was crawling in smaller tunnels. For this reason, I always kept a small flashlight on me. I found all kinds of hiding places in the sewer. Sometimes I would stay down there for hours and then come up a couple miles away from where I started to get away from the cops. The police rarely came into the tunnels after me, but when they did they would never follow me once the tunnels got so small you had to crawl. I would always lose them like this. They figured they would get me the next time.

I had been using meth for eighteen years at this point and only gotten caught with meth once. After that first time getting caught I had only gotten probation. Of course, I skipped out on that and had been on the run with a blue warrant for about a year.

The lights on the police car behind us started flashing. I told the driver to pull over in the parking lot at the four-way stop ahead. She did. As soon as the car stopped, I grabbed my black pouch of dope and started running toward a creek I knew of just across the street. I was headed for a sewer. Unfortunately, police cars were coming from all directions, and there was an officer on foot just a few feet behind me. He yelled out, "I'm going to Tase you!" I could tell by his voice he was close enough to get me for sure. As I ran, I jumped over some bushes, where I discreetly dropped the dope without any of the police noticing. Rather than get Tased, I decided to stop running, allowing myself to get tackled to the ground.

The officer cuffed me up and walked me back to one of the cars. There were at least six cop cars by now. I was feeling pretty good about the whole thing, since I had already ditched the dope and therefore didn't have anything on me. All they could do is get me for violation of probation. I'd go to jail, get my probation reinstated, and then get right back out. Then I noticed the girl who had been driving me was talking to the police. All the police formed a long horizontal line standing side by side and began marching with flashlights in the direction I had run. She had told them that I had dope. When they got to the bushes, they formed a circle, and a couple seconds later they were holding up the dope. I knew it was over. I was going to prison. I remember laying my head back on the seat of the police car and sighing a huge sigh of relief. I knew it was over. I had already made a decision years ago that when I did go to prison I would take the opportunity to clean up and get close to God.

# CHAPTER 21

# INSIDE PRISON

One thing about doing meth and staying up for days at a time over a twenty-year period is that you become very tired. I mean completely and utterly exhausted. You don't realize how bad it is as long as you are still high. Once I got arrested and laid my head back in the police car and sighed in relief, I don't remember much after that until I made it to Tarrant County Jail. I don't remember the drive to North Richland Hills Jail or the time I spent there. I also don't remember the ride from NRH Jail to Tarrant County Jail. I don't remember anything until I had already been in Tarrant County for a few weeks. Do you know why? Because I slept—and slept—and slept. Then I ate and slept, and ate and slept, and ate and slept. I remember feeling glad I was in jail. It felt good to eat and get rest, and I could feel my body getting better. I didn't even care that the food wasn't very good.

Everyone made fun of the "meat" there. There were nicknames for some of it. Names like "Chicken Fried Fake" and "Round Brown." There was one meat that had neon-yellow sauce on it we called "Radioactive Simpson Sauce." I didn't care. I ate mine gladly, along with anyone else's who didn't want theirs. After a couple months I got into a routine, and time started to go a bit faster. I was working out twice a day, gaining weight, and getting in shape quickly.

Then I "caught chain." That meant I was on my way to prison. It was a lot different than jail. Everyone's first stop is a transfer unit. As soon as we got off the bus, the armed guards took all of us into a large room and made us take off all of our clothes. We all stood there naked for a good hour while they searched us. Then they called our names one at a time and sent us to another room where they shaved our heads. Then a shower in front of everyone. No shower curtain. Not even a shower head. Definitely no hot water. Just a hard jet of freezing cold water coming straight out of an open pipe. Afterward, we were sent to another room where we sat naked on cold metal benches for about three hours while we waited for our name to be called to receive a pair of boxer shorts. Soon after, we received a full white uniform, a towel, and a shank-proof toothbrush about two inches long. It was so short you couldn't hold it with your hand. You had to hold it with your thumb and a couple fingers. They say since it is so short it can't be effectively carved into a sharp weapon. I thought this was ridiculous since that same day and every week after they passed out free razors to shave with. Many of those were then taken apart so that the blade could be removed, attached to a comb, and then used to cut hair. A good old comb-and-razor-blade haircut. Honestly, some of the best looking haircuts I've ever seen were done with a comb and razor blade. These blades were repurposed in all kinds of ways. Artists made knives out of them to sharpen their pencils. Other guys made knives for common needs such as cutting string or even food. Because of this, the super-short, shank-proof toothbrush seemed redundant.

One of the first things I noticed that made prison very different from the county jail was that there was no air conditioning. It was an oven. I got to prison in the middle of summer. You would sweat all day and all night. You never did get cool. It took a while to get used to the smell too. What smell? The smell of hundreds of grown men, sweating twenty-four hours a day. It was awful. Tensions ran high all the time. During my first week in the transfer unit, someone got stabbed. He was trying to walk to get help, but he died at the door of the medical building. There were fights all the time.

Most people stayed at the transfer unit around three weeks. You stay very busy being sent to multiple appointments per day with various counselors and other medical staff so they can determine what unit you will go to and serve the remainder of your time. This can be based on your past criminal history, your mental state, your affiliation, and your current behavior. I would definitely say God plays a major role as well. God has been looking out for me my whole life, even though I didn't know it. Now that my heart was in the right place, He began to bless me and show me favor even in prison.

After about three weeks, I was in handcuffs and shackles on a bus again. I was on my way to a very laid-back unit called the Rudd Unit. I believe God orchestrated this. It was a small unit where mostly offenders with drug charges or DWIs were sent. Upon arrival, I was immediately put in front of a panel of three officers who were in charge of assigning new arrivals a job. I sat down. They looked at each other, and one said, "Should we put him in commissary?" That is exactly what they ended up doing. I didn't know it, but I had just gotten blessed with the best job on the whole unit! It was inside and therefore out of the elements. Yes, there was even air conditioning. A prison staff member ran the store, and anywhere the guards or any other prison staff were working, there was air conditioning. So for at least eight hours a day, Monday through Friday, I had air conditioning. The rest of the time, however, I was back in the pod where we actually lived, and there was no air conditioning there.

The windows had bars and were open to the outside. There was a two-month timeframe in which every night around dusk, like clockwork, you could watch out the window as a blanket of thousands of mosquitoes lifted off the ground and started pouring through the windows and into our room. It was so hot that everyone was in just boxer shorts most of the time, so it was impossible not to get bitten. We would be covered in mosquito bites, and the white brick walls would be covered in red blood spots where hundreds of mosquitos were smashed with rubber sandals. There was no mosquito repellent available to us, and so we just had to deal with it every night for about two months. When it got colder, we finally stopped seeing them.

The commissary job also came with a list of other benefits. I got all kinds of extra free food as well as food from outside the unit that no one else got. The hours were good, 8 a.m. to 5 p.m., Monday through Friday. The best part was that with this job I automatically got placed in Building A with a bottom bunk. Building A was the best building there. There were three buildings, A, B, and C. Normally, everyone starts in Building C and works their way up to Building A over time, with a minimum of six months of good behavior. All new people start off with a top bunk and an outside job or an all-night job in the kitchen. Not me. God hooked me up with a good situation right from the start. There were a few people mad about it for sure. I didn't let that bother me.

It didn't take long for me to get settled in. I started a business drawing portraits of my cellmates' family members. They would mostly ask for drawings of their wives and kids. That kept me busy and also kept my locker full of whatever I needed. Coffee, peanut butter, ramen noodle soups, tuna packets, cookies, and of course, more drawing supplies.

I will never forget one of my best memories from when I was locked up. In prison, even the little things matter. Things that are trivial on the outside are sometimes cherished on the inside. Like cereal. In prison, you wait for everything, and I had been waiting a long time for a specific kind of one of those little single-serve, individually packaged cereals. Finally, it came! I was very excited about this and was already planning when I would eat it later that evening. As I started to put it away in my locker under my bunk, my cellmate asked me if he could have some. He was a nice old man from Mexico who knew very little English. I was all about sharing, so I said to him, "Sure, you can have half of it." I was on my way out the door to somewhere, and I left it with him. Later on when I came back, I couldn't find my cereal anywhere. When I asked him where it was, he very innocently said, "You said I could half it." Oh no! Now I understood what had happened. He thought I told him he could have it! Ugh! Well, that day both he and I learned a new word. I learned how to say *half* in Spanish, and he learned the difference between *half* and *have*.

At this point in my life, I was going to church twice a week and reading the Bible multiple times a day. I was even leading nightly prayer and weekly Bible studies. I was eventually offered a place on the praise and worship team and allowed to play guitar twice a week. In my heart, all I wanted to do was the right thing. I felt the best I had in twenty years. I was healthy and strong. I was seeking God and hearing from Him. He never left my side. He is the reason things went so smoothly while I was locked up. I never got into a fight and only came close a couple times. I know He protected me in that way. My dad and mom were visiting me regularly at that point, and I was glad to see them, even under these circumstances.

While I was there, an opportunity came up for me to be baptized in water. I had already been baptized years before, but I felt like I needed to do it again. I wanted to make a new commitment to God, an outward sign of an inward change. I was changed. I was no longer a meth addict, and I would never be one again.

After just under a year, I made parole. I was transferred to Huntsville Unit to be released. This place was like something out of the movies. They unloaded us off the bus and herded us into a large open warehouse-size room with a bunch of chain-length cages inside it. There were broken skylights all over the ceiling, completely open to the outside. Because of this, there were hundreds of pigeons sitting up on beams and rafters. People called this room the birdcage. Do you know what happens when there are hundreds of birds above you? Poop. Lots of poop. People were getting pooped on, and there was nothing we could do about it. This place was crazy! I didn't care, though. I was getting out.

# CHAPTER 22

# WALKING OFF A CLIFF

I will never forget the day I got out. I was sitting in a large room with fifty other guys about to be released. I was mostly quiet and listening to the various conversations going on around the room. Some guys had been locked up for fifteen or twenty years and were finally getting out. I couldn't believe what I was hearing. Those guys who had been in prison for over a decade were talking about how they were about to get high! Some of them had their drug dealers coming to pick them up. Some of them had their same wife or girlfriend picking them up with drugs in hand, ready to get high right then and there! I could not believe it. After so many years, they were going right back to the same thing that got them there.

I remember walking out the door of the prison, which happened to be right in the middle of a town. There were houses and stores across the street. I watched guys get into cars and light up cigarettes and even smoke weed. Other guys walked right across the street and into the gas station and came out with liquor and beer. After years and years of being clean and sober, they went right back to the same things. I envisioned a herd of cattle walking off a cliff. God describes this very thing in the Bible: "Like a dog that returns to his vomit is a fool who repeats his folly" (Proverbs 26:11 ESV).

I want to say now that this is a crucial moment. If you are getting out of prison or rehab after any amount of clean time, you absolutely cannot go back. Not even one time. I can't do meth even one time. If I do, there is no way of knowing if it will be years before I can quit again or if I ever will. Once you are clean, you can never go back. This is one of the biggest mistakes people make. It is not a game. It will take you down faster and harder than ever before. Once you have cleaned your house, which is yourself, and then you make a decision to allow that demon back in your life, he will come back with seven more demons even stronger and more evil than before (see Mathew 12:43–45). You don't stand a chance. "We do not wrestle against flesh and blood, but against principalities, against powers, against the rulers of the darkness of this age, against spiritual hosts of wickedness in the heavenly places" (Ephesians 6:12 NKJV). Stop going about this casually. You are in the fight of your life.

Maybe it's not you. Maybe it's your loved one. Understand that they are in the fight for their life. They had no idea what they were getting into until it was too late. Their heart is still there, intact. They still love you and need you to love them. Pray for them. Pray for their protection. Pray that God will reveal Himself to them. Don't give up, ever. Even if it's been twenty years or thirty years. It's never too late. They can still be saved. They can still change. Even now, I believe God is speaking to some of you with tears running down your face. God is so good, and He hears you and sees you. He loves you, and He loves your sons and daughters. He loves your husbands and wives. He loves you.

CHAPTER 23

# NEW LIFE

When I got out of prison, I had been clean one year. That's the longest I had ever been clean since I started doing drugs twenty years earlier. I was now thirty-four years old. However, I still had a lot of work to do. I had to learn how to live life. I was paroled out to a Christian halfway house called Haven of Rest. There was a woman there named Rachael who also used to be a meth addict, and she owned and ran the place with her husband, who was a pastor. I am so very thankful for their heart to help guys like me. They are amazing people that God uses in a powerful way. I know for sure that when they enter through the gates of heaven someday that God will say, "Well done, good and faithful servant" (Matthew 25:21 NIV). I am honored and blessed to know them. They spend most of their time investing in the guys that come through the halfway house.

Rachael immediately helped me get a job and a ride to and from work. She helped me get $12,000 in tickets reduced to a few hundred dollars. Once that was out of the way, she helped me get a driver's license and a Social Security card. I couldn't believe it. For the first time in many years, I could legally drive! Of course, I didn't have a vehicle yet, but it was coming. My dad wanted to help me with a vehicle. He got me a small truck and let me pay it off. It was a big deal since he had been unable to trust me for many years. I was very thankful. It was the first time anyone had put any kind of trust in me in a very long time. It felt good to be making good choices. One right choice at a time. That's how it works. Each day brought new challenges and tests. I just kept making good choices, one at a time. I watched as men around me fell into temptation and went back to prison. I knew that I could never do drugs again even one time or I would end up just like them.

Rachael helped me get a job immediately after getting out. I was working in a warehouse and driving a forklift. As a felon with no college or even high school education and no special skills, my choices were few. I was making not much more than minimum wage. Regardless, I was determined to do everything different than I did before. I showed up to work every day and did my best.

During this time, I created an account on a Christian dating site. It wasn't long before I met Christina. Once we started talking, we just kept talking. I probably did most of the talking. Either way, one thing led to another, and we met in person to go on a first date. Before long, I was meeting her parents. She was the girl of my dreams, and I was very nervous on the day I actually did meet her parents. We were going to meet them at their house. Christina and I got there a few minutes before them and went in to wait. When they arrived, I jumped up and met them as they were coming in the front door. I went to shake her dad's hand for the first time and knocked his cup of coffee out of his hand and all over the wall. I was so embarrassed! Christina and I would meet up most days from then on, and a few months later we got engaged.

We got married a couple months after getting engaged. We conceived our firstborn son on our wedding night, and around nine months later he was born. I will never forget that moment. As I held him in my arms, I suddenly became aware of two things. The first thing was that I immediately had an unconditional love for my brand-new son unlike any love I had ever had before. The second thing I realized was that my dad must have felt the same way about me. I instantly realized for the first time how much my actions broke his heart. I walked right out to the waiting room in tears, hugged my dad, and told him how sorry I was for all the pain I had caused him. I hugged my mom too and told her the same thing. It was a good healing moment. On multiple occasions over the years I have let them know how sorry I am for everything. It never quite feels like I've said it enough.

As for Christina, she was the wife I had prayed for. God gave me an amazing woman who follows Jesus. To this day, she is an amazing example of what it looks like when you hear from God and follow Him. She is a woman of integrity and has been an inspiration and a rock to me since I met her. She has exceeded all expectations as a wife and mother. All I can say is that I am truly blessed.

CHAPTER 24

# ANYONE CAN START A BUSINESS

Not too long after getting engaged, I felt like God was prompting me to start a lawn service. It was February 2016. The grass wasn't really growing yet, but I felt very strongly that I was hearing correctly. I called Christina from work and told her about it. She asked, "Have you prayed about it?" I told her I would call her right back. I hung up and immediately started to pray and ask God if I was supposed to quit my job. Before I could even get the whole sentence out, I heard, "Yes." I called Christina back and said, "Yep, I'm supposed to quit right now." I let my boss know I was quitting, and I walked out the door.

On my way home, I found a weed eater on the side of the road, and it still worked. It even had a blower attachment. Then, within a day or two, a family friend gave me a push mower. I started going door to door in every neighborhood in a forty-five-minute radius. I would knock and talk to anyone who answered. If they didn't answer, I would leave a handwritten note that said, "I will mow your yard for $20." I would spend eight to ten hours a day looking for lawns to mow. After a few weeks, I already had some repeat business. After a few months, I was making more than I had at any job I had ever had. After the first year, I had to hire a guy to help me. After the second year, I hired multiple guys to help me. In the third year, my wife was able to resign from her corporate job and partner with me in the business. Our revenue almost doubled every year for the first five years.

God blesses everything we do. He gives us favor in every way. God opens door after door after door. We just walk through the doors He opens. He gave us everything we have. We just do our part to keep it. We always do what we say we are going to do. We always do a good job. If we make a mistake, we fix it. We give to others as often and as much as we possibly can. The more we make, the more we give. I want to say now that anyone can start a business and be successful. If I can do it, anyone can. Most people who go to prison believe that once you are a felon, it's over. You can never get a good job and you can never be successful. Or that once you are an addict you are always an addict. None of these statements are true. It doesn't matter how long you have been an addict or if you are a felon. You absolutely can still be successful. I am walking proof. You can have the amazing life you have always dreamed of. A beautiful wife, amazing kids, a successful business, and anything else you can imagine. If you just put in the same amount of effort into starting a new business that you put into being an addict, you will succeed. When I was an addict I did not give up. I did whatever it took to stay high. I did the same with starting a business.

# CHAPTER 25

# MARRIAGE

I would love to say that marriage came easily for me and that we just lived happily ever after, but that is not what happened. My wife has been amazing since the first day. I, however, was not "fixed" just because I went to prison and wasn't doing meth anymore. I always thought that my only real problem was that I was a meth addict. I figured that once the meth was out of the way, I would be fine. It turned out that I had a long list of other horrible issues that would need to be worked out. I was angry, prideful, impatient, insecure, and offended by everything. To top it off, I had a major lust problem. The first six years of my marriage were miserable, mostly for my wife. I went to church and read the Bible and talked the Christian talk, but I was not walking the walk at all. I was mean and short with my wife all the time. I was also in bondage to lust and even pornography. I may have been delivered from meth, but I was still at war. I had no idea I was so messed up.

I felt like I was a toddler learning for the first time how to live a normal life. How to react to and handle normal daily problems. How to react to my wife. How to speak to my wife. How to be in a crowd of people. How to make eye contact with people. How to live a normal life in every way. I had no social skills whatsoever. All those years of drug use caused my brain to be rewired in so many ways. I have spent the last eight years learning how to rewire every area. God says we are to take every thought captive and bring it into submission (2 Corinthians 10:5). Easier said than done, but with daily practice it gets better and easier.

I am very thankful for the woman of God that is my wife. She had to be a very strong and faithful woman to stay with me. It took years of mistakes on my part and then ultimately the worst mistake you can make in a marriage for me to finally open my eyes. It then took a lot of Christian marriage counseling and one-on-one counseling to start the process of repairing our relationship.

If you are a man and reading this, please hear this next part. If you love your wife and in your heart you want to be the husband she needs you to be, please hear me. Let go of your pride. It can't matter who is right any more. It can't matter if what she is saying doesn't make sense to you or doesn't seem logical. It doesn't matter if her feelings don't seem to make sense or seem logical to you. They are still her feelings, and they are real and legitimate to her. It doesn't matter if you think she is wrong. The only thing that matters is that you listen to her and hear her. That's it. She has to feel heard. Even if you don't feel like you have done or said anything wrong, apologize; tell her you are sorry and that you are on her side. This one thing can potentially change the course of your marriage. It doesn't matter who is right. What matters is that you meet her where she is and let her know you care. In addition to this, start praying for your wife every day. It is amazing what God will do. My wife and I now have an amazing relationship and are both so glad we put in the effort to get through the hard times and come out on the other side. She has become the love of my life and my best friend.

CHAPTER 26

# FAMILY RESTORED

G od has done a miraculous work in my life, above and beyond what I ever imagined. My parents—whom I lied to and stole from, whose kitchen I set on fire cooking meth on Christmas Eve, who after years of my drug addiction had no choice but to cut me off completely, who thought I would end up dead in a ditch somewhere—have been completely restored to me. I get to spend time with them, and I am getting to know them. God has even given me the provision to bless them in a variety of ways. That is one of my favorite things to do, since all I did was take from them for twenty years. Even my younger sister and I are talking more and working through the past.

God has strategically put all of the right people in my life to create around me an entire community of people who love me and care about me. He gave me brothers in Christ. He gave me mentors. He gave me my wife and my two boys. He has provided for me spiritually and financially. What God has done for me, I do not deserve. His grace and mercy have humbled me and brought me to my knees. How can I not share my testimony as much as possible for the rest of my life?

CHAPTER 27

# HOW DO I STOP BEING AN ADDICT?

I will be completely straight with you. You don't stop being an addict. Not by yourself. I don't know what you believe at this point in your life. Some of you may completely disregard what I'm about to say. Some of you, though, may be tired. You may be tired of running. Tired of struggling. Tired of being homeless. Tired of being hungry. Tired of being lost and alone. Tired of whatever it is that you don't want to do anymore but can't seem to stop. You try over and over again but do not succeed. You are ready to throw in the towel. Ready to give up. You've tried everything everyone told you would work. Every rehab or every self-help book. Everything the world has to offer. Nothing has worked.

With all of my heart I am telling you: Get down on your knees and with all of your heart ask Jesus to come into your life and save you. Commit your life to Him, and He will save you from any addiction you have. He will save you from yourself. He will save you from your sin. He will walk with you the rest of your life, and He will restore everything that was stolen from you by the enemy. What enemy? The enemy that has been fighting for your soul. The one that has power over you when you are a slave to addiction. A slave to sin. Maybe you've never looked at it like that. Maybe that sounds crazy. Does it, though? Have you not said to yourself, "I'm never going to do this again!" But then you do. Over and over again. What happened to willpower? It doesn't work, does it? There is a power over you when you are bound by sin. In Romans, Paul says, "I do not understand what I do. For what I want to do I do not do, but what I hate I do. . . . But the evil I do not want to do—this I keep on doing" (7:14, 19 NIV). You are in chains. The only one who has the key is Jesus Christ. He can break you free. You have nothing to lose. He wants to save you. He is not willing that any should perish. He loves you more than anything. He loves you so much He sent His only Son to die for you.

I am a walking testimony that this is true. I got down on my face on the floor and screamed and cried out to Jesus, begging for Him to save me, and He did. From that moment, I was saved. My heart changed. I knew that it did. My life was not fixed overnight. I messed up many times after that and even ended up in prison, but God started working things out for my good. He orchestrated circumstances all throughout my life, and one by one my problems were resolved. He began opening doors in my life that I knew could only be Him. He built up my confidence, my courage, and my strength. He molded and is still molding my heart into what it was supposed to be all along. He has blessed me and my family beyond what I had ever dreamed possible in every way. I have a beautiful wife, amazing boys, and a successful business. My family whom I had lost has been fully restored to me.

I am close to ten years clean now. My wife and I are both active members of our church and have both served in leadership positions. I am now traveling to prisons and speaking life and hope into the men there. God is using for the good what the enemy meant to use to destroy me. God is good. I am honored and amazed at what God has done in my life and how He is using my testimony to help others. Even in spite of all the horrible things I have done in my life, God forgave me and gave me a new life. He can and will do the same for anyone.

CHAPTER 28

# ENCOURAGEMENT, EDIFICATION, COMFORT

The Bible says we are to speak life into people. We are to edify and encourage them and lift them up. In this world, people are hurting. They need to know there is hope. They need to know there is a God who sees them, cares about them, and loves them. That is what I hope to accomplish in this book. I want you to know you are loved. There is hope, no matter where you are in life. Maybe you are thinking of committing suicide, and you have asked God, if He is real, to show you a sign. This is it. God is speaking to you right now. He hears you and cares about you. Make a choice to change your mind. Ask Jesus to come into your heart and help you.

Maybe your wife left you. Make a choice right now to humble yourself and allow God to come into your life and change you. Maybe your husband cheated on you. Make a choice right now to ask Jesus to help you forgive him and to save your marriage. Whatever you are struggling with, make a choice right now to give it to God and trust that He can fix it. I have experienced many things in life. Through much pain and many trials, I have learned what is most important in life. After everything is said and done, love is the most important thing in life. When I was homeless and living in the woods, I thought of my family. When I was in fear for my life on the brink of death, I thought of my family. When I was in prison, I thought of my family. When I almost lost my marriage, I thought of my wife and kids. We all know deep down that there is nothing more important than love. We are created with an innate understanding of this truth. The other thing I thought of in each of these instances is God. We are all created with an innate understanding and awareness that there is a God. We all know it deep down. That is why when we experience a life-or-death situation, we automatically start asking God to help us. Even if we never talk to God any other time, we sure speak to Him then.

I say all of this to direct your thoughts in such a way as to remind you of the truth. The devil is a liar. He lies to us, and if we believe his lies, he can dismantle our lives piece by piece until we have nothing left. He will tell us that our marriage is too far gone and can't be saved. He will tell us that we ourselves are too far gone and can't be helped. He will tell us we aren't good enough. Not strong enough. Not smart enough. He will tell us we can't get clean, can't lose weight, can't stop drinking, can't stop doing drugs. He will attack us every step of the way. He will never stop as long as we are alive on this earth. But if we do not believe his lies, he can't touch us. With God, you are good enough. You are smart enough. You are pretty enough. You can stop doing whatever it is that has you enslaved. When you are struggling with whatever it is, just remember what is important at the end of the day. Don't trade what is most important to you for a lie.

You can do this. Find out who God is. Read His Word, the Bible. Talk to Him every day throughout the day, about everything. Before you know it, you will have a relationship with Him. You will feel valued. You will find that you have a purpose. He will open doors in your life, and all you have to do is walk through them. Life is a precious gift. It is short. Years pass by in the blink of an eye. Not even tomorrow is promised. Make every day and every moment count. Spend time with your family. Love God. Love others, and find ways to help people. Encourage, edify, lift up, and comfort people. Just like you needed to hear this, so do others.

We are called to go out into all the world and lead people to Jesus. The only thing that can stop us is ourselves. No matter who you are, you have something to offer. You have gone through something that allows you to help someone else going through the same thing. You may be the one person that someone will listen to. Even more, you may be the one person that actually ends up being in the right place at the right time to save someone. Maybe someone is on their way to commit suicide. Maybe you are the last one that will be in their path. You never know the impact you can have on someone. Just one word or one prayer can make all the difference, even to life or death. We have to care more about saving others than what people might think of us. Who cares what people think?

I want to share a story that my wife and I and her family reflect on often. My wife and I were on a trip with her parents once. It was Christmastime, and we were walking around the downtown area. There were hundreds of people walking everywhere and a lot of traffic. Suddenly we noticed some commotion up ahead. We soon realized that an older gentleman in an electric wheelchair had been hit by a car and thrown out of his wheelchair. The police and ambulance were already on the scene. The man was very belligerent and was refusing all help from the paramedics. He ended up back in his chair and began rolling away, clearly very angry.

I felt an undeniable prompting to go pray for him. I did not want to do that. He was already mad and cursing, and I was sure he did not want to hear from me. It is very easy to convince ourselves that it's not a good time to pray for someone. Or that the circumstance isn't right. Or that they won't listen. Or that it is too late; he is already riding away in his wheelchair. God would not let it go. I told my wife and her parents that I had to pray for him. I ran across the street, caught up to him, and running beside him, I asked him if I could pray for him. He said, "Sure, if you can keep up!" Then he sped up even faster. I started running faster to keep up, and I prayed a full prayer with him, running beside him all the way. By the time I was done, I was out of breath. I'm sure the sight of this whole incident was something to watch. We still laugh about it to this day. My point is this: Don't let anything stop you from doing what God wants you to do. It is all about people. It's all about love. I hope that the testimony of what God has done for me in my life has helped you in your life. With God, all things are possible.

## CHAPTER 29

# CHANGE YOUR NAME

Names are important. Words are powerful. What you believe about yourself matters. What name you have claimed for yourself matters. Even if it's not the truth, if you believe it about yourself then it is truth to you, and you will act accordingly. If you have come to believe that you are an addict, then you are an addict. If you believe you are a loser, then you will probably live up to that name. If you don't believe you can be financially blessed, then you may never be.

For me, my last name was actually spelled *Loser* with a capital *L*. I made a choice when I got out of prison to change my name, literally and legally. I made a choice not to pass that on to my wife or my kids. It's not because of where the spelling of my name came from; it's because of what the world made it. My name is now spelled *Losier*. I am not a loser. I am not an addict anymore. I have been reborn and am a new creation. I am a child of God. "I can do all things through Christ who strengthens me" (Philippians 4:13 NKJV), including making the choice not to do drugs, drink, watch pornography, and so on. It's not about who I was; it's about who I am now in Christ.

I choose not believe the lies of the enemy anymore. He never stops trying, though. He will tell me I'm not smart enough because I didn't go to high school or college. When I'm doing large-scale business deals or when I'm in business meetings with successful companies, he will tell me I'm not good enough because I was a meth addict for twenty years. He will tell me everyone there knows I am different and inferior. When I'm in meetings with ministry leaders, he will tell me I'm not a good enough Christian or that I'm still too sinful to work with these people. These are all lies. We are all just regular people doing the best we can, relying on God's love and grace. You are good enough. No matter what you have done. No matter how many mistakes you made or what they were. God loves you and will forgive you. He is long-suffering, not willing that any should perish (2 Peter 3:9). He wants you to succeed, and He is waiting with open arms for you to run to Him and ask for His forgiveness and for Him to be the Lord of your life. Our Father is so faithful. He is all about our hearts. He is ready to heal all of the hurt and pain in your heart if you will let Him.

If you are an addict or a slave to any sin, pray this prayer with me:

> God, I know that I need You. I can't do this by myself anymore. I am giving You my heart and total control. I am trusting You with my whole life and everything in it. Jesus, I know that You died for me to save me from my sin. I am asking You to come into my heart and change my life. From now on, show me how to live and what Your will is for my life. I love You. Amen.

I was born a Loser, but I was reborn a child of God.

$$\dagger$$

# ACKNOWLEDGMENTS

First and foremost, I owe everything to Jesus Christ for saving me. I was a slave to sin, and He saved me. He also rescued me out of every deep, dark hole that I fell into. He showed me grace and mercy and still does. He has loved me and taught me how to love.

Mom and Dad, I was so worried for so many years that if I ever did get clean it would be too late and that you would already be gone. I am so glad that we get the chance to have a relationship after drugs.

Mom, thank you for never ceasing to pray for me and for never giving up on me. Thank you for giving me food when I was homeless and hungry, even against Dad's wishes. I was hungry and needed the food, and my heart was broken, so I needed to know I was still loved.

Dad, I am glad you are my dad, and I wouldn't want it any other way. I remember seeing the hurt in your face and hearing it in your voice. I'm glad it's over, Dad. I love you.

Lindsay, you are my little sister whom I know I have hurt deeply. I abandoned you for twenty years. Now I am looking forward to working through everything and getting to know you. Though I was lost, now I am found. I am here now.

Christina, you are my loved and cherished wife. My magnet. I couldn't have done this without you. You taught me how to function in this world. You helped me rewire my twisted thought patterns. You helped me see myself the way God does. You are the first woman I've truly loved. You are an exceptional mother and wife. You are a daughter of the Most High. Thank you for your patience and your grace. I have needed it.

Asher and William, you are my best buddies. I am so thankful that you never had to know the old me. I am so very proud of the amazing little boys that you have become. You both bring me indescribable joy. I am truly blessed to have the privilege of being your daddy.

Steve Revel, Jeanette Robert, and Elizabeth Settle, you all have no idea how much you helped me. You helped me to be comfortable in my own skin. You helped me develop the confidence to speak in front of people. You immediately accepted me for who I was and poured into me. You did exactly what you teach. You edified, encouraged, and comforted. Before being under your leadership, I felt inferior around people in church because of my past. You gave me the tools I needed to get past all of that. Now I can share my testimony with the world. Thank you.

Lisa Sewell, you were the single most valuable and important factor that God used to launch our business into the commercial side of landscaping. You and all of the networking that resulted because of you put us on the map. It can all be traced back to you and your willingness to give us a chance. Thank you for all you have done and for being the amazing friend you have become.

Jack the Ripper, you were my dog. You were just a puppy when I got you. I rescued you from that horrible motel. But really, I needed you too. You were my only friend. I am so sorry for all of the freezing cold and rainy nights I had you outside with me. I am sorry that I had to go to prison and give you up. I am sure you thought I abandoned you or didn't want you anymore. That's not true. You are a good dog, and I love you. I'm so thankful that my parents took you in and that you have a good home.

## Other Books From Dove Publishing House

*Kingdom Authority*
By Beth Williams

*I Teach World Changers*
A Prayer Devotional for Teachers
By Monica Lemke

*Wings*
A College Girls Devotional
By Jennifer Weiss

*Holy Spirit Adventures*
God at Work in the Marketplace
By Jennifer Weiss

*Joy in the Morning*
A Sixty-Day Devotional
By Kym Keck

*Something Beautiful, Something Good*
From Darkness to the Light of Christ
By Pamela Gillins

www.dovepublishinghouse.com

Cory Losier and his wife, Christina, have a heart to see the captives set free. If you would like to schedule Cory to speak or be a part of prison ministry, please reach out. Bulk orders of 12 or more books for small groups and prison ministry are available at a discounted price via the following email address: DitchtoDestiny@gmail.com

The Spirit of the Sovereign Lord is on me, because the Lord has anointed me to proclaim good news to the poor. He has sent me to bind up the brokenhearted, to proclaim freedom for the captives and release from darkness for the prisoners.
Isaiah 61:1 NIV

Made in the USA
Columbia, SC
15 April 2025

56690308R00054